THE BUDDHA

the buddha

writings on the enlightened one

edited by tom morgan

foreword by lama surya das

photographs by glen allison

new world library
novato, california

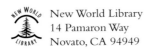
New World Library
14 Pamaron Way
Novato, CA 94949

Library of Congress Cataloging-in-Publication data available
upon request.

First printing, October 2002
ISBN 1-57731-227-9
Printed in Korea
Distributed to the trade by Publishers Group West
10 9 8 7 6 5 4 3 2 1

Page 2–3: Kyaukhpyugyi Paya (700 years old), Nyaungshwe, Inle
lake, Myanmar (Burma).

Page 4: Gold Buddha's face, Sha Tin, New Territories, Hong Kong.

Page 8: Buddhist altar, Wat Hai Sok, Vientiane, Laos.

Opposite: Detail of Buddha's enlightenment (ninth century).
From the great stupa of Borobudur in Java. It has the earth-
touching pose of hands (bhumisparsa-mudra).

Pages 10–11: Kyaukhpyugyi Paya (700 years old), Nyaungshwe,
Inle lake, Myanmar (Burma).

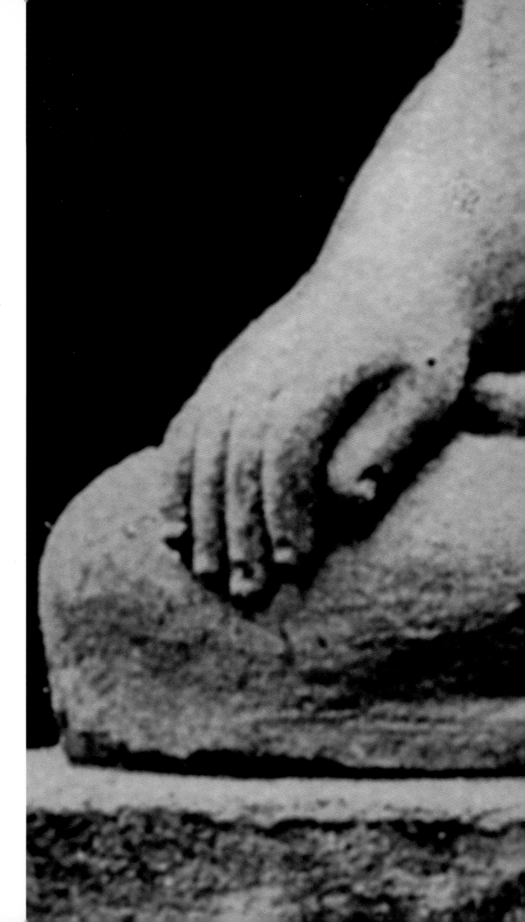

contents

Foreword Lama Surya Das

The first time I crossed the threshold of a Buddhist temple, my jaw dropped. It was just so unspeakably peaceful: everything perfectly at rest. What a mystery, what a blessing, what a surprise! I had reached the end of the path at the very outset, however fleetingly, and for an eternal instant, I felt my whole world slip away—one true taste of the holy now, a lifetime experienced in that one moment. Who knew what more the Buddha would have in store for me?

At twenty years old, I had no intention of becoming a Buddhist. I was on the road, seeking to find what I was looking for in life, not even knowing what it was. The Buddhist temple that I had entered was located at the Ladkhi Vihara in bustling Old Delhi. It was the tail end of the turbulent sixties. But at that moment, for all I knew I was in another world, another dimension, another life.

It felt as if I had come home. Standing inside the dim, candlelit, incense-laden temple, I looked into the serene eyes of the Buddha statue, and the Buddha looked at me. For the very first time in my life, I felt understood and as if I actually belonged in a house of worship. Not that I comprehended or even felt attracted to the elaborate images and accouterments of the Tibetan temple around me, but Lord Buddha and I seemed to understand each other. That sweet feeling has persisted for over thirty years now. I occasionally wonder when this sacred honeymoon period might wear off!

I find inspiration, blessings, teaching, and guidance every single day through the Buddha, his teachings, and the sacred Buddhist community. It explains why I have taken refuge in the Triple Gem. There is never a time when I do not find peace and freedom by sitting down in front of a statue or an image of the enlightened Buddha, my teacher. As far as I can tell, Lord Buddha remains alive and well.

Not a god or an avatar, Buddha was a saintly human teacher who showed the way to enlightenment, a state of being that he himself had discovered during six long years of arduous yoga and meditation in the wilderness. Buddha's "gift that keeps on giving" is that he taught us how to traverse

13

Opposite: Shwedagon Paya (Pagoda), Yangon (Rangoon), Myanmar (Burma).

Above: Detail of Tibetan thangka painting.

the same path that he himself traveled. Buddhism, as it is practiced in many countries today, is a way of life grounded in the Buddha's own enlightenment experience and his subsequent teachings on how to realize spiritual liberation ourselves. It remains a tried and true method of spiritual deliverance. Thus, the Buddha's life has become extraordinarily significant. Through its guiding principles, intention, and practices, as well as in each of its external details, it has become a model for us all to emulate.

Our human life is meaningful in its particulars, as well as in the universality it may achieve when lived for something greater than itself. The life of the compassionate Buddha is an excellent example of this. His is the story of a human being who achieved the fullest flowering of his humanity. In the role of enlightened teacher, torchbearer, guide, Way-opener, and social reformer, the Buddha helped and continues to help millions of others to also experience their true, full, and radiant nature.

According to tradition, the Buddha had not just one but many lives dedicated to the altruistic mission of achieving enlightenment for the benefit of all living things. Tradition tells us that he recalled and recounted five hundred such lives—each one lived as a bodhisattva lives— in which he developed on the path to full enlightenment. Some of these stories are contained here in the Jataka Tales, but all of Buddhism derives from the life, lifestyle, teaching, investigative methods, logic, and example of the one historical Buddha Gautama. The Buddha represents and personifies enlightenment—Buddhahood—something anyone can realize by following the spiritual path of awakening to its ultimate consummation.

The Buddha lived in India and entered nirvana reclining on his right side beneath a tree over two millennia ago, on the full moon in May during the year 483 B.C.E. It was the culmination of a long and productive eighty-year life. However, the authentic Buddha is beyond coming and going, life and death—a timeless, immutable, universal principle, and an embodiment of total awareness and here-and-now wakefulness. His life reminds us of what we are all capable of accomplishing.

I think this is what I love most about Buddhism: it speaks directly to me—to us—across time and distance. The truth is that I don't always comprehend the message, but at least I know it is for me. I love the vitality and accessibility of Buddha's perennial wisdom, directly transmitted in the form of oral Dharma teachings from the living masters, along with the close and supportive kinship I experience among its sincere practitioners. I intuitively feel this truth, beyond my ordinary mind and intellectual understanding, and I can immerse myself in it without reliance on creed or dogma.

I have known many Buddhist masters, including my own Tibetan lama teachers, spiritual mentors who lived the life of a Buddha, both in the East and in the West, right in the middle of the twentieth century. They modeled an exemplary way of being in the world, yet remained not entirely of the world,

and they brought forth wisdom and love by being of service to all around them. They taught me how to find the meaning and higher purpose of my own life, through meditation, contemplation, and spiritual inquiry. I am grateful for this, and I feel that direct experience (however fleeting) of the fruits (however small) of Buddhist practice has transformed my life and my understanding of this world and of eternity, of the nature of time and space and the universe, and also my relations to others and to this gritty world.

Buddha opened my heart and mind. I have learned patience, acceptance, and trust from his living example. Sometimes, when I feel at a loss, I like to simply bow or lower my head, have a moment of mindfulness and prayer, and listen for that still, small, quiet voice deep inside, as I ask, "What would Buddha do?" Please don't think I am boasting if I confide that I have never yet been let down. This is why I bring it all to the Buddha, every day, and even every moment—if and when I can remember to be mindful enough to do so. When I bow daily before Buddha, I try to look into who is Buddha, as well as who and what I am. Exactly who is bowing to whom? When no one is bowing to no one and nothing, this is true reverence; authentic bowing then begins, and the life of the Buddha is reenacted. Buddhist practices, even one as simple as bowing, has outer, inner, and innermost levels of meaning, and cannot be judged merely by appearances. For example, it might look like a meditator is practicing by themselves, but their practice is not just for themselves.

Buddhahood is the realization of Mind Essence, the true nature of heart and mind. This spiritual awakening known as enlightenment is the sole goal of Buddhism; it is practiced and actualized by developing wisdom and compassion through Buddha's Three Liberating Trainings: ethical self-discipline, meditative awareness, and wisdom. This we see expressed in Lord Buddha's iconic life, which functions like a beacon to those of us who are oriented in that way. We are all Buddhas by nature; all we have to do, spiritually speaking, is to live in accordance with the Three Trainings, awaken from illusion's sleep, and realize who and what we truly are. That is enlightenment, spiritual illumination, and self-realization. The sublime peace, deathless ease, wisdom, and freedom of enlightenment are what Buddhism has to offer a benighted world today. This treasure trove is available within. Help yourself.

Until the Communist onslaught in the early and middle decades of the last century, Buddhism was the most populous religion in the world. Buddhism is older than Christianity and Islam. The Buddha is said to have taught 84,000 Dharmas. Much of his vast and profound spiritual teaching remains extant today, for the benefit of one and all. Yet wherever the Dalai Lama travels around the world, he tells audiences not to rush to become Buddhists, but, rather, that Buddhist practice can help one become a better whatever-you-are: Jew, Christian, Muslim, Humanist, or Agnostic. Moreover, the Dalai Lama has exhorted Buddhist teachers to "contribute to others rather than to convert others." I find this peaceful,

non-proselytizing, tolerant message of spiritual brotherhood most appropriate for today.

Buddhism is an entire universe of its own. Not unlike other religions, Buddhism has its own cosmology, geography, rites and rituals, liturgies and scriptures and commentaries, pilgrimage places, saints and sinners, hagiographies and original literary genres, philosophy and metaphysics, psychology, astrology, health and healing sciences, architecture, art and iconography, music and dance, as well as its renowned meditation, chanting, and yoga practices. There are a multitude of Buddhist traditions, schools, sects, lineages, practices, and styles in the many different countries and regions of this Dharma world. The long-ago day when I entered that temple, and thus, the world of Buddhism, was the happiest day of my life—besides today. This is why I am a Buddhist; Dharma practice brings me joy, meaning, inner peace, and harmony. I can only wish for everyone the same felicity in their spiritual pursuits.

It is an honor to be asked to write an introduction to an anthology about the life of the Buddha. The learned and distinguished international contributors to this book are well qualified to present the historical story, message, meaning, and significance of Buddha's life, including its relevance today, both to us individually and to our society at large. Here will be found traditional teachings and selections from heart of the Buddhist classics such as the Dhammapada; teachings on the nature of reality and the liberating practices of mindfulness, nonviolence, and loving-kindness from the Buddha's renowned Noble Eightfold Path and Four Liberating Truths; and also the impact of modern applications of Dharma, as seen in the essay on Buddhism and "death row."

I have confined myself here to writing a personal introduction to the timeless spiritual life and ever-present being of the Buddha, as I know it. Spirituality is nothing if it is not personal, an intimate matter of body, mind, and spirit. Buddhism has a very large heart. I have traveled to meditate in the holy sites sacred to Buddhism, and I am assured that what is there is also right here, where we are—where you are. The timeless Buddha, the Buddha-nature, lives within you. I have shared my story as an offering along the way of awakening. May the life of Buddha prove beneficial to all, as it has for me.

Sarvamangalam. May all beings be peaceful and free.

1. Siddhartha Gotama
A VERY BRIEF BIOGRAPHY

WALPOLA SRI RAHULA
from *What the Buddha Taught*

The Buddha, whose personal name was Siddhartha (Siddhārtha in Sanskrit), and family name Gotama (Skt. Gautama), lived in North India in the sixth century B.C.E. His father, Suddhodana, was the ruler of the kingdom of the Sākyas (in modern Nepal). His mother was queen Maya. According to the custom of the time, he was married quite young, at the age of sixteen, to a beautiful and devoted young princess named Yasodhara. The young prince lived in his palace with every luxury at his command. But all of a sudden, confronted with the reality of life and the suffering of mankind, he decided to find the solution—the way out of this universal suffering. At the age of twenty-nine, soon after the birth of his only child, Rahula, he left his kingdom and became an ascetic in search of this solution.

For six years the ascetic Gotama wandered about the valley of the Ganges, meeting famous religious teachers, studying and following their systems and methods, and submitting himself to rigorous ascetic practices. They did not satisfy him. So he abandoned all traditional religions and their methods and went his own way. It was thus that one evening, seated under a tree (since then known as the Bodhi- or Bo-tree, 'the Tree of Wisdom'), on the bank of the river Neranjara at Buddha-Gaya (near Gaya

23

Opposite: Japanese postcard Buddha, circa 1936. Above: The Miracle of Sravasti.
Sandstone. Fifth century C.E. Sarnath, India.

in modern Bihar), at the age of thirty-five, Gotama attained Enlightenment, after which he was known as the Buddha, 'The Enlightened One'.

After his Enlightenment, Gotama the Buddha delivered his first sermon to a group of five ascetics, his old colleagues, in the Deer Park at Isipatana (modern Sarnath) near Benares. From that day, for forty-five years, he taught all classes of men and women— kings and peasants, Brahmins and outcasts, bankers and beggars, holy men and robbers—without making the slightest distinction between them. He recognized no differences of caste or social groupings, and the Way he preached was open to all men and women who were ready to understand and to follow it.

At the age of eighty, the Buddha passed away at Kusinara (in modern Uttar Pradesh in India).

Today Buddhism is found in Ceylon (Sri Lanka), Burma (Myanmar), Thailand, Cambodia, Laos, Vietnam, Tibet, China, Japan, Mongolia, Korea, Formosa (Taiwan), in some parts of India, Pakistan, and Nepal, and also in the (former) Soviet Union. The Buddhist population of the world is over 500 million.

"The Buddha . . . was not a religious fanatic, attempting to act in accordance with some high ideal. He just dealt with people simply, openly, and very wisely. His wisdom came from transcendental common sense. His teaching was sound and open."
— Chögyam Trungpa, *Cutting Through Spiritual Materialism*

26

2. The Brahmin's Son
SIDDHARTHA IS DISCONTENT AND BEGINS A QUEST

HERMANN HESSE
from *Siddhartha,* his novel of the Buddha's life

In the shade of the house, in the sunshine on the riverbank by the boats, in the shade of the sallow wood and the fig tree, Siddhartha, the handsome Brahmin's son, grew up with his friend Govinda. The sun browned his slender shoulders on the riverbank, while bathing at the holy ablutions, at the holy sacrifices. Shadows passed across his eyes in the mango grove during play, while his mother sang, during his father's teachings, when with the learned men. Siddhartha had already long taken part in the learned men's conversations, had engaged in debate with Govinda, and had practiced the art of contemplation and meditation with him. Already he knew how to pronounce Om silently—this word of words, to say it inwardly with the intake of breath, when breathing out with all his soul, his brow radiating the glow of pure spirit. Already he knew how to recognize Atman within the depth of his being, indestructible, at one with the universe.

There was happiness in his father's heart because of his son who was intelligent and thirsty for knowledge; he saw him growing up to be a great learned man, a priest, a prince among Brahmins.

There was pride in his mother's breast when she saw him walking, sitting down, and rising: Siddhartha—strong, handsome, supple-limbed, greeting her with complete grace.

Opposite: One of the fifty-three towers in the structure known as the Bayon, Cambodia. Above: Detail of Tibetan thangka painting, Buddha of Healing.

Love stirred in the hearts of the young Brahmins' daughters when Siddhartha walked through the streets of the town, with his lofty brow, his king-like eyes, and his slim figure.

Govinda, his friend, the Brahmin's son, loved him more than anybody else. He loved Siddhartha's eyes and clear voice. He loved the way he walked, his complete grace of movement; he loved everything that Siddhartha did and said, and above all he loved his intellect, his fine ardent thoughts, his strong will, his high vocation. Govinda knew that he would not become an ordinary Brahmin, a lazy sacrificial official, an avaricious dealer in magic sayings, a conceited worthless orator, a wicked sly priest, or just a good stupid sheep amongst a large herd. No, and he, Govinda, did not want to become any of these, not a Brahmin like ten thousand others of their kind. He wanted to follow Siddhartha, the beloved, the magnificent. And if he ever became a god, if he ever entered the All-Radiant, then Govinda wanted to follow him as his friend, his companion, his servant, his lance bearer, his shadow.

That was how everybody loved Siddhartha. He delighted and made everybody happy.

But Siddhartha himself was not happy. Wandering along the rosy paths of the fig garden, sitting in contemplation in the bluish shade of the grove, washing his limbs in the daily bath of atonement, offering sacrifices in the depths of the shady mango wood with complete grace of manner, beloved by all, a joy to all, there was yet no joy in his own heart. Dreams and restless thoughts came flowing to him from the river, from the twinkling stars at night, from the sun's melting rays. Dreams and a restlessness of the soul came to him, arising from the smoke of the sacrifices, emanating from the verses of the Rig-Veda, trickling through from the teachings of the old Brahmins.

"You know what Buddha did? He was married, he was the son of a maharaja. He had a harem, a son, a wife. . . . But when he was thirty years old he became very melancholy. He didn't even look at the dancing girls any more. They said, 'What's the matter with you? The dancing girls are so beautiful.' He said, 'If these girls are so beautiful now, they'd stay beautiful. They wouldn't grow old . . . die . . . become corrupt . . . decay . . . fall apart.' He said, 'I gotta get out of here and find some way to stop all this.' He was deeply unhappy. He had to sneak out at night on a white horse. He cut all his golden hair off—he had long, blond hair—he was an aryan, you know, an aryan Indian. And he cut off his long, blond hair and he sat in the woods amid peace, and he found out that the cause of suffering was *birth!* If we hadn't been born, none of all this would have happened. Oh, yes, that the cause of suffering, of grief, of decay, and of death is simply birth. So, he also discovered that the world didn't really exist, and it doesn't exist, except in some relationship to the form of being, which fits me perfectly."

—Jack Kerouac,
in an interview with Alfred G. Aronowitz,
in the October 1960 issue of *Escapade*

Siddhartha had begun to feel the seeds of discontent within him. He had begun to feel that the love of his father and mother, and also the love of his friend Govinda, would not always make him happy, give him peace, satisfy and suffice him. He had begun to suspect that his worthy father and his other teachers, the wise Brahmins, had already passed on to him the bulk and best of their wisdom, that they had already poured the sum total of their knowledge into his waiting vessel; and the vessel was not full, his intellect was not satisfied, his soul was not at peace, his heart was not still. The ablutions were good, but they were water; they did not wash sins away, they did not relieve the distressed heart. The sacrifices and the supplication of the gods were excellent—but were they everything? Did the sacrifices give happiness? And what about the gods? Was it really Prajapati who had created the world? Was it not Atman, He alone, who had created it? Were not the gods forms created like me and you, mortal, transient? Was it therefore good and right, was it a sensible and worthy act to offer sacrifices to the gods? To whom else should one offer sacrifices, to whom else should one pay honor, but to Him, Atman, the Only One? And where was Atman to be found, where did He dwell, where did His eternal heart beat, if not within the Self, in the innermost, in the eternal which each person carried within him? But where was this Self, this innermost? It was not flesh and bone, it was not thought or consciousness. That was what the wise men taught. Where, then, was it? To press towards the Self, towards Atman—was there another way that was worth seeking? Nobody showed the way, nobody knew it—neither his father, nor the teachers and wise men, nor the holy songs. The Brahmins and their holy books

The Biggest Daibutsu in Japan dates from 749 and the height is 53 1/2 feet and the face being 16 feet long at Nara

knew everything, everything; they had gone into everything—the creation of the world, the origin
of speech, food, inhalation, exhalation, the arrangement of the senses, the acts of the gods. They knew
a tremendous number of things—but was it worthwhile knowing all these things if they did not know
the one important thing, the only important thing?

Many verses of the holy books, above all the Upanishads of Sama-Veda spoke of this innermost
thing. It is written: "Your soul is the whole world." It says that when a man is asleep, he penetrates his
innermost and dwells in Atman. There was wonderful wisdom in these verses; all the knowledge of
the sages was told here in enchanting language, pure as honey collected by the bees. No, this tremendous
amount of knowledge, collected and preserved by successive generations of wise Brahmins could not
be easily overlooked. But where were the Brahmins, the priests, the wise men, who were successful
not only in having this most profound knowledge, but in experiencing it? Where were the initiated
who, attaining Atman in sleep, could retain it in consciousness, in life, everywhere, in speech and in
action? Siddhartha knew many worthy Brahmins, above all his father—holy, learned, of highest esteem.
His father was worthy of admiration; his manner was quiet and noble. He lived a good life, his words
were wise; fine and noble thoughts dwelt in his head—but even he who knew so much, did he live
in bliss, was he at peace? Was he not also a seeker, insatiable? Did he not go continually to the holy
springs with an insatiable thirst, to the sacrifices, to books, to the Brahmins' discourses? Why must he,
the blameless one, wash away his sins and endeavor to cleanse himself anew each day? Was Atman then
not within him? Was not then the source within his own heart? One must find the source within one's
own Self, one must possess it. Everything else was seeking—a detour, error.

These were Siddhartha's thoughts; this was his thirst, his sorrow.

He often repeated to himself the words from one of the Chandogya-Upanishads. "In truth, the
name of Brahman is Satya. Indeed, he who knows it enters the heavenly world each day." It often

seemed near—the heavenly world—but never had he quite reached it, never had he quenched the final thirst. And among the wise men that he knew and whose teachings he enjoyed, there was not one who had entirely reached it—the heavenly world—not one who had completely quenched the eternal thirst.

"Govinda," said Siddhartha to his friend, "Govinda, come with me to the banyan tree. We will practice meditation."

They went to the banyan tree and sat down, twenty paces apart. As he sat down ready to pronounce the Om, Siddhartha softly recited the verse:

"Om is the bow, the arrow is the soul,
Brahman is the arrow's goal
At which one aims unflinchingly."

When the customary time for the practice of meditation had passed, Govinda rose. It was now evening. It was time to perform the evening ablutions. He called Siddhartha by his name; he did not reply. Siddhartha sat absorbed, his eyes staring as if directed at a distant goal, the tip of his tongue showing a little between his teeth. He did not seem to be breathing. He sat thus, lost in meditation, thinking Om, his soul as the arrow directed at Brahman.

Some Samanas once passed through Siddhartha's town. Wandering ascetics, they were three thin worn-out men, neither old nor young, with dusty and bleeding shoulders, practically naked, scorched by the sun, solitary, strange and hostile—lean jackals in the world of men. Around them hovered an atmosphere of still passion, of devastating service, of unpitying self-denial.

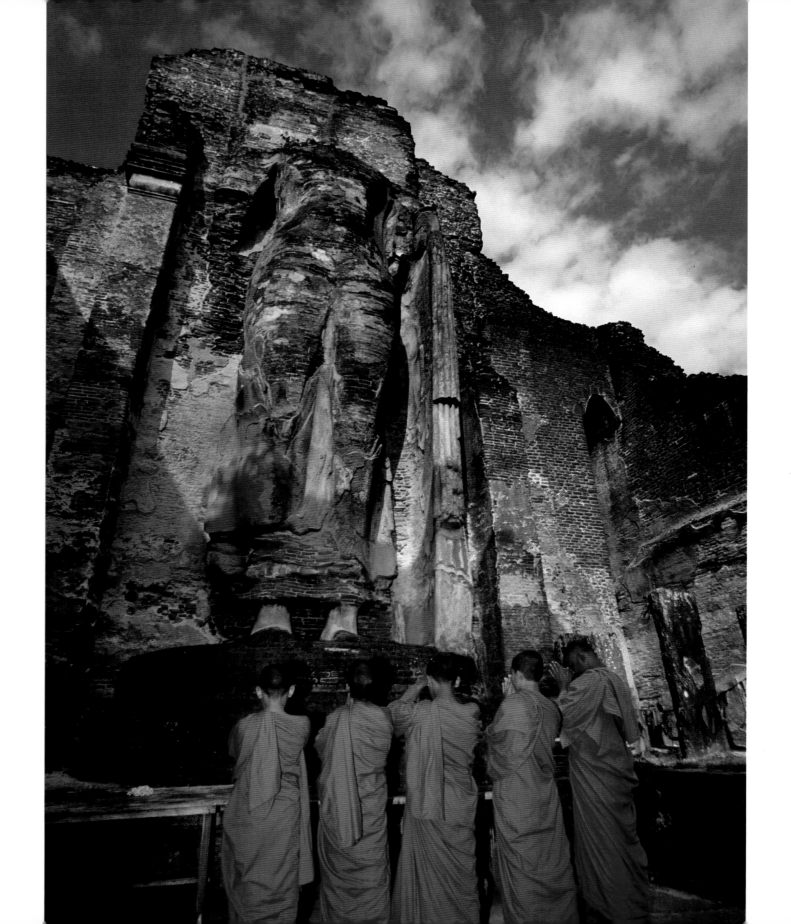

In the evening, after the hour of contemplation, Siddhartha said to Govinda: "Tomorrow morning, my friend, Siddhartha is going to join the Samanas. He is going to become a Samana."

Govinda blanched as he heard these words and read the decision in his friend's determined face, undeviating as the released arrow from the bow. Govinda realized from the first glance at his friend's face that now it was beginning. Siddhartha was going his own way; his destiny was beginning to unfold itself, and with his destiny, his own. And he became as pale as a dried banana skin.

"Oh, Siddhartha," he cried, "will your father permit it?"

Siddhartha looked at him like one who had just awakened. As quick as lightning he read Govinda's soul, read the anxiety, the resignation.

"We will not waste words, Govinda," he said softly. "Tomorrow at daybreak I will begin the life of the Samanas. Let us not discuss it again."

Siddhartha went into the room where his father was sitting on a mat made of bast. He went up behind his father and remained standing there until his father felt his presence. "Is it you, Siddhartha?" the Brahmin asked. "Then speak what is in your mind."

Siddhartha said: "With your permission, Father, I have come to tell you that I wish to leave your house tomorrow and join the ascetics. I wish to become a Samana. I trust my father will not object."

The Brahmin was silent so long that the stars passed across the small window and changed their design before the silence in the room was finally broken. His son stood silent and motionless with his arms folded. The father, silent and motionless, sat on the mat, and the stars passed across the sky. Then his father said: "It is not seemly for Brahmins to utter forceful and angry words, but there is displeasure in my heart. I should not like to hear you make this request a second time."

The Brahmin rose slowly. Siddhartha remained silent with folded arms.

"Why are you waiting?" asked his father.

"You know why," answered Siddhartha.

His father left the room displeased and lay down on his bed.

As an hour passed by and he could not sleep, the Brahmin rose, wandered up and down, and then left the house. He looked through the small window of the room and saw Siddhartha standing there with his arms folded, unmoving. He could see his pale robe shimmering. His heart troubled, the father returned to his bed.

As another hour passed and the Brahmin could not sleep, he rose again, walked up and down, left the house, and saw the moon had risen. He looked through the window. Siddhartha stood there unmoving, his arms folded; the moon shone on his bare shinbones. His heart troubled, the father went to bed.

He returned again after an hour and again after two hours, looked through the window, and saw Siddhartha standing there in the moonlight, in the starlight, in the dark. And he came silently again, hour after hour, looked into the room, and saw him standing unmoving. His heart filled with anger, with anxiety, with fear, with sorrow.

And in the last hour of the night, before daybreak, he returned again, entered the room, and saw the youth standing there. He seemed tall and a stranger to him.

"Siddhartha," he said, "why are you waiting?"

"You know why."

"Will you go on standing and waiting until it is day, noon, evening?"

"I will stand and wait."

"You will grow tired, Siddhartha."

"I will grow tired."

"You will fall asleep, Siddhartha."

"I will not fall asleep."

"You will die, Siddhartha."

"I will die."

"And would you rather die than obey your father?"

"Siddhartha has always obeyed his father."

"So you will give up your project?"

"Siddhartha will do what his father tells him."

The first light of day entered the room. The Brahmin saw that Siddhartha's knees trembled slightly, but there was no trembling in Siddhartha's face; his eyes looked far away. Then the father realized that Siddhartha could no longer remain with him at home—that he had already left him.

The father touched Siddhartha's shoulder.

"You will go into the forest," he said, "and become a Samana. If you find bliss in the forest, come back and teach it to me. If you find disillusionment, come back, and we shall again offer sacrifices to the gods together. Now go, kiss your mother and tell her where you are going. For me, however, it is time to go to the river and perform the first ablution."

He dropped his hand from his son's shoulder and went out. Siddhartha swayed as he tried to walk. He controlled himself, bowed to his father, and went to his mother to do what had been told to him.

As, with benumbed legs, he slowly left the still sleeping town at daybreak, a crouching shadow emerged from the last hut and joined the pilgrim. It was Govinda.

"You have come," said Siddhartha and smiled.

"I have come," said Govinda.

3. Enlightenment

KAREN ARMSTRONG
from *Buddha*

We do not know how long it took Gotama to recover his health after his years of asceticism. The scriptures speed up the process to make it more dramatic, and give the impression that Gotama was ready for the final struggle with himself after one bowl of junket. This cannot have been true. The effects of mindfulness and the cultivation of skillful states take time. Gotama himself said that it could take at least seven years, and stressed that the new self developed imperceptibly over a long period. "Just as the ocean slopes gradually, falls away gradually, and shelves gradually with no sudden incline," he later warned his disciples, "so in this method, training, discipline, and practice take effect by slow degrees, with no sudden perception of the ultimate truth." The texts show Gotama attaining his supreme enlightenment and becoming a Buddha in a single night, because they are less concerned with historical fact than with tracing the general contours of the process of achieving release and inner peace.

Thus in one of the oldest portions of the scriptures, we read that after Gotama had been deserted by his five companions and had been nourished by his first meal, he set off toward Uruvela, walking there by easy stages. When he reached Senānigāma beside the Nerañjara river, he noticed "an agreeable plot of land, a pleasant grove, a sparkling river with delightful and smooth banks, and, nearby, a village whose inhabitants would feed him." This, Gotama thought, was just the place to undertake the final

Opposite: German book cover for *Sculpture of India* from 1921 depicting Buddha's enlightenment. Above: Detail of Tibetan thangka painting.

effort that would bring him enlightenment. If he was to reproduce the calm content that had modulated so easily into the first *jhana* under the rose-apple tree, it was important to find a congenial spot for his meditation. He sat down, tradition has it, under a bodhi tree, and took up the *asana* position, vowing that he would not leave this spot until he had attained Nibbana. This pleasant grove is now known as Bodh Gaya and is an important site of pilgrimage, because it is thought to be the place where Gotama experienced the *yathabhuta*, his enlightenment or awakening. It was in this spot that he became a Buddha.

It was late spring. Scholars have traditionally dated the enlightenment of Gotama at about the year 528 B.C.E., though recently some have argued for a later date in the first half of the fifth century. The Pāli texts give us some information about what happened that night, but nothing that makes much sense to an outsider who has not been through the Buddhist regimen. They say that Gotama mused upon the deeply conditional nature of all life as we know it, saw all his past lives, and recovered that "secluded" and solitary state he had experienced as a child. He then slipped easily into the first *jhana*, and progressed through ever higher states of consciousness until he gained an insight that forever transformed him and convinced him that he had freed himself from the round of *samsara* and rebirth. But there seems little new about this insight, traditionally known as the Four Noble Truths and regarded as the fundamental teaching of Buddhism. The first of these verities was the noble truth of suffering (*dukkha*) that informs the whole of human life. The second truth was that the cause of this suffering was desire (*tanha*). In the third noble truth, Gotama asserted that Nibbana existed as a way out of this predicament and finally, he claimed that he had discovered the path that leads from suffering and pain to its cessation in the state of Nibbana.

47

There seems nothing strikingly original about these truths. Most of the monks and ascetics of North India would have agreed with the first three, and Gotama himself had been convinced of them since the very beginning of his quest. If there is anything novel, it was the fourth truth, in which Gotama proclaimed that he had found a way to enlightenment, a method which he called the Noble Eightfold Path. Its eight components have been rationalized still further into a threefold plan of action, consisting of morality, meditation, and wisdom:

[1] *Morality (sila)*, which consists of right speech, right action, and right livelihood. This essentially comprises the cultivation of the "skillful" states in the way we have discussed.

[2] *Meditation (samadhi)*, which comprises Gotama's revised yoga disciplines, under the headings of right effort, mindfulness, and concentration.

[3] Wisdom (pañña): the two virtues of right understanding and right resolve enable an aspirant, by means of morality and meditation, to understand the Buddha's Dhamma, enter into it "directly" and integrate it into his or her daily life in the way that we shall discuss in the following chapter.

If there is any truth to the story that Gotama gained enlightenment at Bodh Gaya in a single night, it could be that he acquired a sudden, absolute certainty that he really *had* discovered a method that would, if followed energetically, bring an earnest seeker to Nibbana. He had not made this up; it was not a new creation or an invention of his own. On the contrary, he always insisted that he had simply discovered "a path of great antiquity, an ancient trail, traveled by human beings in a far-off, distant era."

The other Buddhas, his predecessors, had taught this path an immeasurably long time ago, but this ancient knowledge had faded over the years and had been entirely forgotten. Gotama insisted that this insight was simply a statement of things "as they really are"; the path was written into the very structure of existence. It was, therefore, *the* Dhamma, par excellence, because it elucidated the fundamental principles that govern the life of the cosmos. If men, women, animals, and gods kept to this path, they could all attain an enlightenment that would bring them peace and fulfillment, because they were no longer struggling against their deepest grain.

But it must also be understood that the Four Noble Truths do not present a theory that can be judged by the rational intellect alone; they are not simply notional verities. The Buddha's Dhamma was essentially a method, and it stands or falls not by its metaphysical acuity or its scientific accuracy, but by the extent to which it works. The truths claim to bring suffering to an end, not because people subscribe to a salvific creed and to certain beliefs, but because they adopt Gotama's program or way of life. Over the centuries, men and women have indeed found that this regimen has brought them a measure of peace and insight. The Buddha's claim, echoed by all the other great sages of the Axial Age, was that by reaching beyond themselves to a reality that transcends their rational understanding, men and women become fully human. The Buddha never claimed that his knowledge of the Four Noble Truths was unique, but that he was the first person, in this present era, to have "realized" them and made them a reality in his own life. He found that he *had* extinguished the craving, hatred, and ignorance that hold humanity in thrall. He had attained Nibbana, and even though he was still subject to physical ailments and other vicissitudes, nothing could touch his inner peace or cause him serious mental pain. His method had worked. "The holy life has been lived out to its conclusion!" he cried out triumphantly at the end of that momentous night under the bodhi tree. "What had to be done has been accomplished; there is nothing else to do!"

Those of us who do not live according to the Buddhist program of morality and meditation have, therefore, no means of judging this claim. The Buddha was always quite clear that his Dhamma could not be understood by rational thinking alone. It only revealed its true significance when it was apprehended "directly," according to yogic methods, and in the right ethical context. The Four Noble Truths do make logical sense, but they do not become compelling until an aspirant has learned to identify with them at a profound level and has integrated them with his own life. Then and only then will he experience the "exultation," "joy," and "serenity" which, according to the Pali texts, come to us when we divest ourselves of egotism, liberate ourselves from the prison of self-centeredness, and see the Truths "as they really are." Without the meditation and morality prescribed by the Buddha, the Truths remain as abstract as a musical score, which for most of us cannot reveal its true beauty on the page but needs to be orchestrated and interpreted by a skilled performer.

Even though the Truths make rational sense, the texts emphasize that they did not come to Gotama by means of discursive reasoning. As he sat meditating under the bodhi tree, they "rose up" in him, as from the depths of his being. He apprehended them within himself by the kind of "direct knowledge" acquired by a yogin who practices the disciplines of yoga with "diligence, ardor and self-control." Gotama was so absorbed in these Truths, the object of his contemplation, that nothing interposed itself between

them and his own mind and heart. He had become their human
embodiment. When people observed the way he behaved and
responded to events, they could see what the Dhamma was like; they
could see Nibbana in human form. In order to share Gotama's
experience, we have to approach the Truths in a spirit of total self-
abandonment. We have to be prepared to leave our old unregenerate
selves behind. The compassionate morality and yoga devised by Gotama
only brought liberation if the aspirant was ready to lay aside all egotism.
It is significant that at the moment he achieved Nibbana under the
bodhi tree, Gotama did not cry "I am liberated," but "It is liberated!"
He had transcended himself, achieved an *exstasis,* and discovered an
enhanced "immeasurable" dimension of his humanity that he had not
known before.

What did the new Buddha mean when he claimed to have reached
Nibbana on that spring night? Had he himself, as the word implied,
been "snuffed out," extinguished like a candle flame? During his six-year quest, Gotama had not masochisti-
cally courted annihilation but had sought enlightenment. He had wanted to wake up to his full potential
as a human person, not to be wiped out. Nibbana did not mean personal extinction: what had been
snuffed out was not his personality but the fires of greed, hatred and delusion. As a result, he enjoyed
a blessed "coolness" and peace. By tamping out the "unhelpful" states of mind, the Buddha had gained
the peace which comes from selflessness; it is a condition that those of us who are still enmeshed in
the cravings of egotism, which make us hostile toward others and distort our vision, cannot imagine.

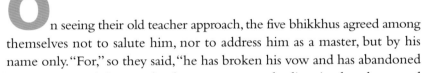

On seeing their old teacher approach, the five bhikkhus agreed among themselves not to salute him, nor to address him as a master, but by his name only. "For," so they said, "he has broken his vow and has abandoned holiness. He is no bhikkhu but Gotama, and Gotama has become a man who lives in abundance and indulges in the pleasures of worldliness."

But when the Blessed One approached in a dignified manner, they involuntarily rose from their seats, and greeted him in spite of their resolution. Still they called him by his name and addressed him as "friend Gotama."

When they had thus received the Blessed One, he said: "Do not call the Tathagata by his name nor address him as 'friend,' for he is the Buddha, the Holy One. The Buddha looks with a kind heart equally on all living beings, and they therefore call him 'father.' To disrespect a father is wrong; to despise him, is wicked.

"The Tathagata," the Buddha continued, "does not seek salvation in austerities, but neither does he for that reason indulge in worldly pleasures, nor live in abundance. The Tathagata has found the middle path.

"There are two extremes, which the man who has given up the world ought not follow—the habitual practice, on the one hand, of self-indulgence which is unworthy, vain, and fit only for the

Opposite: Walking Buddha. Stucco.

Above: Buddha giving benediction. Stone. Wat Raw, Ayudhya, Thailand.

worldly-minded—and the habitual practice, on the other hand, of self-mortification, which is painful, useless, and unprofitable.

"Neither abstinence from fish or flesh, nor going naked, nor shaving the head, nor wearing matted hair, nor dressing in a rough garment, nor covering oneself with dirt, nor sacrificing to Agni will cleanse a man who is not free from delusions.

"Reading the Vedas, making offering to priests, or sacrifices to the gods, self-mortification by heat or cold, and many such penances performed for the sake of immortality, these do not cleanse the man who is not free from delusions.

"Anger, drunkenness, obstinacy, bigotry, deception, envy, self-praise, disparaging others, superciliousness, and evil intentions constitute uncleanness; not the eating of flesh.

"A middle path, avoiding the two extremes, discovered by the Tathagata—a path which opens the eyes, and bestows understanding, which leads to peace of mind, to the higher wisdom, to full enlightenment, to Nirvana!

"What is that middle path, avoiding these two extremes, discovered by the Tathagata—that path which opens the eyes, and bestows understanding, which leads to peace of mind, to the higher wisdom, to full enlightenment, to Nirvana?

"Let me teach you the middle path, which keeps aloof from both extremes. By suffering, the emaciated devotee produces confusion and sickly thoughts in his mind. Mortification is not conducive even to worldly knowledge; how much less to a triumph over the senses!

"He who fills the lamp with water will not dispel the darkness, and he who tries to light a fire with rotten wood will fail. And how can any one be free from self by leading a wretched life, if he does not succeed in quenching the fires of lust, if he still hankers after either worldly or heavenly pleasures. But he in whom self has become extinct is free from lust; he will desire neither worldly nor heavenly

pleasures, and the satisfaction of his natural wants will not defile him. However, let him be moderate, let him eat, and drink according to the needs of the body.

"Sensuality is enervating; the self-indulgent man is a slave to his passions, and pleasure-seeking is degrading and vulgar. But to satisfy the necessities of life is not evil. To keep the body in good health is a duty, for otherwise we shall not be able to trim the lamp of wisdom, and keep our mind strong and clear. Water surrounds the lotus-flower, but does not wet its petals.

"This is the middle path that keeps aloof from both extremes."

And the Blessed One spoke kindly to his disciples, pitying them for their errors, and pointing out the uselessness of their endeavours, and the ice of ill-will that chilled their hearts melted away under the gentle warmth of the Master's persuasion.

Now the Blessed One set the wheel of the most excellent law rolling, and he began to preach to the five bhikkhus, opening to them the gate of immortality, and showing them the bliss of Nirvana.

The Buddha said: "The spokes of the wheel are the rules of pure conduct: justice is the uniformity of their length; wisdom is the tire; modesty and thoughtfulness are the hub in which the immovable axle of truth is fixed. He who recognizes the existence of suffering, its cause, its remedy, and its cessation has understood the four noble truths. He will walk in the right path.

"Right views will be the torch to light his way. Right aspirations will be his guide. Right speech will be his dwelling-place on the road. His gait will be straight, for it is right behaviour. His refreshments will be the right way of earning his livelihood. Right efforts will be his steps; right thoughts his breath; and right contemplation will give him the peace that follows in his footprints.

"Now, this is the noble truth concerning suffering:

"Birth is attended with pain, decay is painful, disease is painful, death is painful. Union with the unpleasant is painful, painful is separation from the pleasant, and any craving that is unsatisfied, that

Left: Medicine Buddha. Detail of Tibetan thangka painting.
Opposite: Row of Buddha statues, Wat Suthat, Bangkok,
Thailand.

too is painful. In brief, bodily conditions which spring from attachment are painful.

"This, then is the noble truth concerning suffering.

"Now this is the noble truth concerning the origin of suffering:

"It is that craving which causes the renewal of existences, accompanied by sensual delight, seeking satisfaction now here, now there, the craving for the gratification of the passions, the craving for a future life, and the craving for happiness in this life.

"This, then is the noble truth concerning the origin of suffering.

"Now this is the noble truth concerning the destruction of suffering:

"It is the destruction, in which no passion remains, of this very thirst; it is the laying aside of, the being free from, the dwelling no longer upon this thirst.

"This, then is the noble truth concerning the destruction of suffering.

"Now this is the noble truth concerning the way which leads to the destruction of sorrow. it is this noble eightfold path; that is to say:

"Right views; right aspirations; right speech; right behaviour; right livelihood; right effort; right thoughts; and right contemplation.

"This, then is the noble truth concerning the destruction of sorrow.

"By the practice of loving kindness I have attained liberation of heart, and thus I am assured that I shall never return in renewed births. I have even now attained Nirvana."

"In seeking the Buddha, seeking the Dharma, seeking so-called enlightenment, one imposes an extra head on top of one's own. The Zen expression 'Kill the Buddha!' means to kill any concept of the Buddha as something apart from oneself. To kill the Buddha is to *be* the Buddha."
— Peter Matthiessen, *Nine-Headed Dragon River*

And the Blessed One had thus set the royal chariot-wheel of truth rolling onward, a rapture thrilled through all the universes.

The devas left their heavenly abodes to listen to the sweetness of the truth; the saints that had parted from life crowded around the great teacher to receive the glad tidings; even the animals of the earth felt the bliss that rested upon the words of the Tathagata: and all the creatures of the host of sentient beings, gods, men, and beasts, hearing the message of deliverance, received and understood it in their own language.

And when the doctrine was propounded, the venerable Kondannya, the oldest one among the five bhikkhus, discerned the truth with his mental eye, and he said: "Truly, O Buddha, our Lord, thou hast found the truth!" Then the other bhikkhus too, joined him, and exclaimed: "Truly, you are the Buddha, you have found the truth."

And the devas and saints and all the good spirits of the departed generations that had listened to the sermon of the Tathagata, joyfully received the doctrine, and shouted: "Truly, the Blessed One has founded the kingdom of righteousness. The Blessed One has moved the earth; he has set the wheel of Truth rolling, which by no one in the universe, be he god or man, can ever be turned back. The kingdom of Truth will be preached upon earth; it will spread; and righteousness, good-will, and peace will reign among mankind."

5. Stories of the Buddha

BUDDHIST VALUES AND MORALS ILLUSTRATED IN PARABLES

The Mosquito Jataka

(MAKASA-JATAKA)

"BETTER a foe."—This the Teacher told at a village while on tour among the Magadhese, about villagers who were fools. It is said that the Tathâgata, having once gone from Savatthi to the kingdom of Magadha and there making a tour, reached a certain hamlet. That hamlet was usually noted for the blind folly of its men. There such men had one day come together and taken counsel, saying "Masters, when we go and work in the forest, mosquitoes bite us, and on that account we have to knock off work. Let's take our bows and weapons and wage war on mosquitoes; hitting and chopping we shall have killed all the mosquitoes." They went into the forest, and saying "We shall hit the mosquitoes," they hit and struck each other, and much hurt they came back and laid down in the village and in the marketplace and at the gate.

The Teacher, with his train of monks, entered that village for alms. The residue of wise men, when they saw him, made a pavilion at the gate, made many offerings, and saluting him took seats. The Teacher, seeing wounded men here and there, asked those laymen: "Many are the folk that ail; what have they done?" "Reverend sir, these men, saying 'We will wage war on the mosquitoes,' went and wounded each other. They've made themselves ill." The Teacher, saying "Not now alone have those blindly foolish men thinking to strike mosquitoes struck themselves; in the days gone by also

Opposite: Gold Buddha, Sha Tin, New Territories, Hong Kong.

Above: "Sangye Menla." Medicine Buddha of Healing. Stained glass thangka created by Ani Thubten Jamyang Donma.

there were men who, saying 'We'll strike the mosquito,' became strikers of another man"; and begged by the men he brought up the past.

In the past, when Brahmadatta was reigning at Benares, the Bodhisat was making his living by trade. Then, in a border village in the kingdom of Kasi, many woodcraftsmen were living. And there a bald man was planting a tree. Now a mosquito alighted on his head, which shone like the black of a copperplate, and as if it had been a blow from a dart wounded him with its jaws. He said to his son seated by: "Tata, a mosquito is wounding my head as if it were hitting me with a dart." "Tata, hold steady, I'll kill it with a blow." And just then the Bodhisat, in quest of business, had arrived at that village and was seated in the woodcraftsman's workshop. Then the woodcraftsman said to his son: "Tata, stop this mosquito!" He, saying "I'll stop it, Tata," raised a sharp axe and, standing behind his father—"I'll hit the mosquito"—broke his father's head in two. The woodcraftsman there and then died.

The Bodhisat, seeing that action, thought, "Better is a wise foe for he will not kill from fear of men's vengeance," and he said this verse:

"Better an enemy who's won some sense,
Than friend of any sense bereft.
The silly babbler says 'I'll slay the gnat!'
And breaks his father's topmost limb."

Saying this verse, the Bodhisat arose and went according to his deeds, and the kinsmen of the woodcraftsmen did their duty by the body.

The Teacher . . . joined on the series and assigned the Jataka: "Then the wise trader who spoke and went away was just I."

The Monkey-Lord Jataka
(VANARINDA-JATAKA)

"IN whom are these four things."—This the teacher told while living at the Bamboo Wood about Devadatta's going about to kill him. "Not only now, monks," said he, "does he do so; he did so in the olden days also, but he was not able to destroy me." And he brought up the past.

In the past, when Brahmadatta was reigning at Benares, the Bodhisat, reborn in the monkey world, and in course of growth become as big as a colt and very strong, dwelt on the bank of a river. In the middle of the river was a little island, fertile in divers fruit trees such as mangoes, bread fruit, and the like. The Bodhisat, being as strong as an elephant, would leap from his bank and alight on a flat rock, lying midway between his bank and the islet, and thence leap over to the isle. There he would eat his fill of fruit and then return in the evening, and on another day do the same. By this method he kept himself alive.

Now at this time there was a crocodile and his consort living in that river. And the wife, seeing that Bodhisat go by time after time, lusted after his heart's flesh, and told her mate of her craving. The crocodile said, "Very good, you shall get it," and thinking, "To-day as he comes back at evening from the island I'll catch him," he went and lay down on the flat rock. The Bodhisat, having spent the day on the island, stood there in the evening and looked over to the rock, and he thought: "That rock appears higher to-day, what's the reason?" For he used to determine the height of the water and of the rock, and thus it occurred to him: "To-day there is neither fall nor rise in the height of the water, yet the rock has become bigger; I wonder now whether there's a crocodile living on the rock to catch me? I'll first test him." And standing there as if talking with him, he said: "Master rock!" After three calls, getting no reply, he said: "Rock!" The rock showed no response. Then the monkey said: "Why, master

73

rock, is it that to-day you make no reply?" The crocodile thought, "Why sure, on other days this rock has been giving answer to the monkey; I'll now answer him," and he said: "What is it, master monkey?" "Who are you?" "I am a crocodile." "What are you lying there for?" "Hoping I'll get your heart's flesh." The Bodhisat thought: "There's no other way for me to go; to-day I'll have to get round that crocodile." And he said to him: "Good crocodile, I'll give myself up to you; open your mouth and catch me as I come." Now crocodiles, when their mouths are open, shut their eyes. This is what happened with this crocodile, he not seeing the plan. And so he lay. The Bodhisat, seeing how he was, mouth open, eyes shut, sprang from the island on to the crocodile's head, and thence, like a flash of lightning, leapt again and alighted on the riverbank. The crocodile, seeing the feat, thought, "It's a marvel this monkey has done," and saying, "Master monkey, a man in this world who has four things overcomes his enemies; all four are inside you, I reckon," spoke this verse:

"In whom are these four things, lord monkey, as in you,
Truth, right, resolve, surrender, he outruns the foe."

Thus praising the Bodhisat, the crocodile went to his own place.

The Teacher then assigned the Jataka: "Then the crocodile was Devadatta, his wife was the young Brahminee Chincha, but the monkey-lord was just I."

The Advantage in Morality Jataka
(SALÂNISAMSA-JATAKA)

"BEHOLD of faith."—This the Teacher told when living at the Jetavana about a believing layman. This elect disciple, a convinced believer, was going, they say, one day to the Jetavana, and coming by eventide to the banks of the Achiravati, the ferrymen having beached their boat that they might go to the service, and he seeing no boat at the landing-stage, grasped the thought of Buddha as ecstasy and was crossing the river. His feet did not sink in the water. Going as if on land, when he got to midstream he saw waves, whereupon his ecstatic Buddha-thought grew weak, and his feet began to sink. But, strengthening the ecstasy, he went on the water's surface, and entering the Jetavana saluted the Teacher and sat down at his side. The Teacher making him welcome asked him: "Layman, did you come along your way without much trouble?" And he saying "Reverend sir, grasping the Buddha-thought as ecstasy, I won footing on the water's surface, as if I were pressing the earth, and so came," he said: "Layman, it is not only you who remembering the Buddha-virtues won footing, in bygone days, too, laymen, shipwrecked in open sea, remembering Buddha-virtues, won footing." And being asked about it he brought up the past.

In the past, in the day of the Very Buddha Kassapa, a converted worthy disciple embarked on a ship, together with a land-owning barber. The barber's wife had committed him to the layman's hands, saying, "Sir, his welfare and ill is your burden." In a week that ship was wrecked in mid-ocean. And those two lying on a plank reached a little island. There the barber killing birds cooked them and eating gave to the layman. The layman, saying "Enough! (not) for me!" did not eat; but he was thinking, "In this place there is no other foothold save the three refuges," and recollected the virtues of the three gems.

77

Then, as he recollected and recollected, a Naga (cobra) king, born in that little island, transformed his own body into a great ship. A sea-deva became the pilot. The ship was filled with the seven kinds of gems. The three masts were of sapphire, the sail was of gold, the ropes were silver, the planks were golden. The sea-deva, standing on board, called out: "Anyone for Jambudipa?" The layman said: "We are." "Well, then, come aboard!" He went on board and summoned the barber. The sea-deva said: "You are allowed, not he." "Why?" "There's no moral quality or conduct in him; that's why. I brought the ship for you, not for him." "Let be; I, in my own gifts given, moral code warded, practices practiced, give accomplishment to him." The barber said: "Master, I thank you!" The deva, saying "Now I'm going," made him come aboard, and bringing them both from off the sea, and going by river to Benares, by his power deposited money in the house of each. Commending associating with the wise, he said, "One should keep company with the wise. If this barber had not kept company with this layman, he had been destroyed in mid-ocean," and he said the verse:

> "Behold of faith, of morals and of generosity this fruit:
> A serpent in ship's form bears home the pious layman.
> With the good consort, make yourselves intimate with the good.
> By the company of the good it was, the barber saved."

Thus the sea-deva standing in the air admonished, teaching the right, then catching hold of the serpent went to his own mansion.

The Teacher . . . assigned the Jataka: "Then the converted layman was one who passed beyond life; the Naga king was Sariputta, the sea-deva was just I."

6. Letter to Beverly

KEROUAC ATTEMPTS TO EXPLAIN THE BRIGHT ESSENTIAL NEWS OF BUDDHISM

JACK KEROUAC — A BUDDHIST LETTER / JAN. 2, 1955
from *Some of the Dharma*

Dear Bev,

In answer to your request "Write me something to think about" let me attempt to explain the Teaching of the Buddhas of Old to you, so that you can join me in the gradual happiness, and liberation that comes with wholehearted sincere understanding of the mysterious law of things as elucidated & unfolded more times than there are grains of sand in the sea, to living beings in this world, and all others in the ten directions in and out of the created universe, by Buddhas and Great Bodhisattvas, and humble disciples like myself too, always without regard for self-profitable consequence but for the sake of revealing to some other living being trapped in this world of suffering the path that leads out of the confusion and the nightmare, to the permanent awakening of bliss and perfect loving-kindness in the realization of the truth of Mind Essence.

Not that you're wanting in love, sweet Beverly, as any of us who know you, religious and unreligious alike, do purely testify; and not that you're scarce in kindness, the way you heap riches of affection and cook for everybody and spend your hard-earned money in every direction all the time. But now I want to unfold to you the principle that teaches that human love incorporates and gives form to the beams of Enlightenment itself, but does form last?

Form changes and disappears, but the essence remains.

81

Opposite: Brahma, King of the Heavenly Hosts. Japanese. Eighth century.
Dry lacquer sculpture in the Hokke-do of Todai-ji, Nara, Japan.
Above: Detail of Tibetan thangka painting.

So that you'll know, when your present body vanishes, and your form returns to its origin in nothingness, this love vanishes not. Because it comes from the perfect love of Mind Essence, which abides before, and during and after form, and since form comes and goes like a phantom, then form is imaginary.

So if you heap sweet riches of generousness on me, say a steak dinner, or wine, or a kiss with your lips, be it known:- steaks come and go, wines come and go, but the perfect love of Mind Essence which manifested itself through these gifts in this world of forms, neither comes nor goes.

Beverly, the teaching of the truth is this perfect love of Mind Essence is everywhere permeating throughout forms and space all over, and is indeed the very substantiality, the very suchness, of both forms and space; it's what the world is made of.

Perfect Love of Mind Essence is what there is, amen—or in Sanskrit, Om; or in French, ainsi soit il, meaning, Thus it is.

And thus it is.

Now as my chosen words thread onwards, crowds of confusion fall around them, and I have to explain and make clear what is meant by perfect love of Mind Essence. And the only reason why I forced myself, a really cold loveless Breton Canuck, to begin on the subject of love, was because I was conscious of your womanhood and your inevitable natural infatuation with love, your deep immense immersion in the subject of love, your attachment to love, your love of love, and your very answer to my last letter when I said "What is there to say?" and you said "Oh hell, love!"

But when perfect love of Mind Essence becomes the love among forms, because of that contamination, because of that descent from perfection of essence to imperfection of form, suffering arises.

And it's for the reason of showing you the way out of suffering, not to question your sweet love in suffering human form, that I want to unfold the Teaching of Old to you.

Further, too, I want you to discard in your mind any notions of my own suffering human form, which is as phantasmal, brief and impermanent as your own. It isnt that we've grown old and come to thoughts of the impermanency of our lives, but rather that from the moment of birth our lives were automatically on the way out, in the first place and from the first dewy moment.

But forget me as the Jack that you know, because these words don't have their origin in "Jack" or in any form with a name, these words have been similar to the selfsame words and signs devised by the Buddhas of Old and to Come to be regarded solely as forms pointing to the truth of Mind Essence, not to be regarded as the suchness of the perfect Love of Mind Essence itself. So as I seek to point at essence for you, dont take the form, the finger, to be the essence.

If you do that, you'll take the finger, the form, the words, to be the essence, while all the time essence (shall we say) is Unpointable.

And also by discarding all thoughts of me as "Jack," you will see that I'm not real and never was; that I had no selfhood, just as you; that my body and my form were fleeting things; that living beings are like fishes arising and dying in the Great Sea, which is as their essence.

Fishes hatching from eggs, appearing, suffering, dying and disappearing again. Where did they come from? Where did they go? But the saying is, the sea rolls on.

And where went the loving of the fishes? And where went the hating of the fishes? And where went the thinking of the fishes? And these forms went back to essence.

To make sure you won't be attached to this Teaching, as being in the possession of, originating from, or being delivered by, a person such as "Jack," therefore, was mentioned the advisability of discarding the form and conception of a "Jack." Take this, rather, as the Teaching mysteriously transmitted from the unknown, as it was to "me," solely due to the efforts and activity of the Buddhas and Tathagatas,

Opposite: Detail of Jade Buddha Temple
(interior), Shanghai, China.

who are no-beings and no-forms and so are in possession of the perfect love of Mind Essence continuously and without contaminations.

As you have been, and are, and always will be intrinsically in highest truth a Buddha too.

II

What is Mind Essence? and what is Buddhahood?

Buddhahood is the realization of Mind Essence.

Mind Essence is what you'll realize this minute if you just stop everything and close your eyes and sit still, let your body relax and forget it's there, and listen to the silence. Soon, in a minute, you'll open your eyes and leave behind the contemplation of the Milky Way in your eyelids and the whole world will reappear to your sight like an eerie dream.

In remembering your body again, you'll shift limbs or blow your nose or scratch an itch which in itself is imaginary. You'll start thinking of what to eat, what it will taste like. But you'll suddenly remember that food eaten in dreams always has that single Mind-taste. From outside come noises, shattering into the silent shh of your silence like pebbles rippling up a cool pool.

The cool pool was the inside ceaseless hearing of your Mind Essence; now the forms of noises, like pebbles, break up the calm mirror. So you know Mind in its Essence is like a mirror. How beautiful it is that a mere form can suddenly realize its essence! This is Buddhahood, if only for a second; and have you ever seen a cat sitting on folded paws, with eyes like slits, completely still, ignoring all cat-calls and even caresses and all disturbances? Anyone rushing up to this cat and picking him up, what has he done? The animal had fallen into a trance of contemplation, had successfully realized the world

"The first line of Mumon's verse reads: 'A dog, Buddha-nature'—there is no need for 'nature.' 'A dog is Buddha'—'is' is superfluous. 'A dog, Buddha'—still redundant. 'Dog!'—that's enough! Or just 'Buddha!' You have said too much when you say 'A dog is Buddha.' 'Dog!'—that is all. It is completely Buddha."
— Roshi Philip Kapleau, *The Three Pillars of Zen*

away, discarded the dream even to the blissful calm of ignoring all sounds rising or arisen and all responses via the pricking of the supersensitive ears. This person has committed a blunder grabbing the cat.

But when the cat is asleep and twitching from a nightmare, ah then pick him up and wake him up; the blunder becomes forgiveness.

Beverly, I discuss the cat because I want you to realize that all living beings, including cats, are different forms of Mind. That's why the Buddhas never say "human beings" they say "sentient beings," beings of sense possessing six senses and therefore beings under punishment of the pain of death; and so that's why the highest perfect wisdom of the Buddhas reaches not only into all kingdoms of existence on this earth, but all kingdoms of existence in all the ten thousand directions of unnumbered mighty chilicosms throughout everwhere.

What do you think? If a monster on Mars a million years ago held still for a second and realized by virtue of its essential motivity and mentality that its form was just a form buried lonely and sufferingly in the Great Sea of essential Mentality, which he certainly could see, if he had eyes, by looking at the endless empty sky above, then what's absurd about saying that our little sentient cat realized his own essence? (I say that Buddhahood is the religion of all living beings in all kingdoms of existence because it is Indian, and the very earth is an Indian thing. For instance, Beverly, the Pomo Indians of California had this to say of the "whites" their conquerors from West Europe who came with cross and sword: 'They don't know that everything is alive.' This is my personal observation, that wherein it is possible to realize that the Essence of Things never has changed, that it was not Essence that took shape but Ignorance that took the shape, all living creatures on all levels of physical size can know it and attain Tathagatahood (Essencehood).)

Because when we say "sentient beings" we also say Buddhahood, for without sentient beings and their forms of ignorance, there could be no Buddhas and the essence of enlightenment. What would

89

Opposite: Standing Buddha at Wat Intharawihan, Bangkok, Thailand.

there be to enlighten? What need is there to enlighten empty space? But even an ant is sentient and is a pitiful form of ignorance, even an ant is a different form of Mind, though small and "unimportant" by our "human" worldly standards.

But how big a monster is an ant to a germ? How big a monster is a germ that you can see through a microscope, to a germ that you can't see through a microscope? How is this germ built? Like the universe, atom-like, a few planets revolving around a central neutron, on down into the germ and on out into the universe we live in and the Universe of that.

So you'll know the whole created universe is swarming everywhichway with sentient forms of all sizes all buried in suffering, each form in a state of ignorance, though the essence has never changed and never will, and therefore each form is potentially in a state of enlightenment of No-Form, by realization of its original essence which is the perfect solitude of the unbornness of the unborn essence of all things which is like the perfect solitary lovelight of Love of Mind Essence.

III

You sit again and close your eyes, and cross your legs underneath you in the traditional rock-like & stalwart position for meditation initiated by the human sages of the East because of its unmovability and nerve-calming effect, though you might just as well be standing at a subway strap, and again you sink deep in a quiet Stop-Everything of your outside suffering form. You let it melt away, ignoring the dream of life for an examination of the mind itself that makes the dream appear, or in which the dream seems to appear.

Because there's nothing there but emptiness and essence, no figures, forms, shapes, pictures, you get scared and want to return to the life of the world.

91

Buddha, seventh century. Wood. Nara, Japan.

At times, worse, you can't stop the pictures and thoughts, like watching a movie on a screen. But because it's like a movie on a screen, you realize the movie itself is unreal phantasms and the screen is the only reality.

The "screen" is your Mind Essence, the movie is forms that come and go.

Suddenly someone disconnects the plug and the movie vanishes like a flash, like a bubble burst, like a dream, and all's left is the White Screen snowy perfect like the Bright Room of Holy Gold in the middle of the Mind. But what can you do with an empty screen, you've got to think, move, act, eat, "live."

So you return to the world, you yourself become a movie on the Screen of the Sole Reality, and go in search of your poor sentient needs, such as food, rest, even companionship. Let's say you go see a movie about monkeys.

But now you know that when the monkeys were swinging from branch to branch in the movie, they were not really there, just apparitions on the screen, and they were not really swinging from branch to branch; it was of the least importance to you before to consider this.

You've realized the utter unreality of not only the monkeys, monkeys indeed, but the utter unreality of any conception as to whether they really exist or not, exist indeed.

In your worldly mind you'll ponder and smile, and say "Well, of course the monkeys were photographed, their apparitions in various shades of brightness and darkness were preserved in film, and now they were just projected on this white screen, and so I saw them, and at least I know they were real once."

But Beverly! real indeed! How could they be photographed in the first place, if it wasnt for their forms? And how could brightness and darkness manifesting the shadows of their forms be preserved on film, if it wasnt for their forms?

93

"Since it will be said, it's an old picture and all the
monkeys are dead and gone, where were these
monkeys before they were undead and ungone?
Monkeys, monkeys indeed; dead, dead indeed; gone,
gone indeed; forms, forms indeed."

Supposing the camera instead had been pointed at the empty sky? And how could they now be projected on a white screen from a film, if it wasnt for the shadowy preservation of the shadows of their forms? Where were their forms before they had forms? Where shall their forms be after they've had their forms?

And where are their forms now that they have their forms?

Their forms are shadows on the Universal Great Film of Essence of Mind, reflections of monkeys merely. The essence is not changed, monkeys are nothing but figures of speech we have.

You dont believe it? But from where came, and where going, and why dont their forms remain and be real?

Since it will be said, it's an old picture and all the monkeys are dead and gone, where were these monkeys before they were undead and ungone?

Monkeys, monkeys indeed; dead, dead indeed; gone, gone indeed; forms, forms indeed.

It's because of our own serious mistake of consciousness which is called Ignorance, of which Mind is not the Cause because Mind is intrinsically empty and pure but Ignorance within itself takes the Initiative and appears unto itself, i.e., appears in the minds of sentient beings everywhere, that there exists the illusion of the monkeys. Whether you wished to specify it as God's Mind or as Universal Storage Mind (Alaya-Vijnana), there is one door of Purity and Enlightenment and Nirvana, it seems, and there is the other door of Defilement and Ignorance and Sangsara, it seems; and in Reality and High Truth, neither door exists, nothing exists, that is to say, neither nothing or something but beyond that simply Neither and Not-Neither Together. Blur your focus, cross your eyes, look at the liquid world waver and vanish.

If Ignorance ended, so would the illusion of existence, but how can the Essence of the ignorance and of the illusion ever end? The Essence never had a beginning, never will end, and really is not to

be considered at all but completely forgotten, that is, as an object of "thought" and "memory." The Essence of Universal Mind which is what you see, smell, hear, taste, feel and think about everywhere you may be, and you may be everywhere, but yet you have never seen the essence, nor smelt it, nor heard it, nor tasted it, nor felt it, nor thought of it, you only made these contacts with Ignorance.

It's because of this and other explanations, poor as the explanations are, that we can say the monkeys arent even, werent even ever real:- Supposing I went out in the yard and took six fistfuls of air and came in the house and created a SLAT, in my childish simplicity.

Or, which is essentially the same, I took six sticks and nailed them together and called it a SLAT then I turn around and say, "Before, ladies and gentlemen, in all ten quarters of the Universe, this SLAT did not exist.' But as to even the existence or non-existence of the SLAT, what could be more absurd and trivial? It's only a figure of speech, a manner of speaking. If we had no brains we couldnt say the SLAT "existed"; the rock says the SLAT "exists"?

This is the created world and all its monkeys.

And now I say, "The SLAT exists." This too is just a figure of speech.

And then, when the SLAT, because put-together by me and only because in my ignorance put-together by me, inevitably falls apart, and even the very sticks turn to dust and finally to energy and finally to nothingness, it will be said "The SLAT no longer exists." This too is just a figure of speech, words about some shadowy form that was a no-form and became a no-form again and in between held an empty "existence" the essence of which was also No Form (in Truth).

SLAT, SLAT indeed.

Opposite: Sakyamuni in meditation, Murozi Temple.

Above: Buddha from Central Asia. T'ang Dynasty.

The same with its representation, say, on film; we photograph the bloody slat; the same with the pitiful film itself. The film is made of emptiness, photograph it with microscopic atomic cameras and nothing's there. These are all confused fancies and eerie dreams of "form-seemingness" inside the sick mind working on one another and creation various visions and medleys of looks, in what is intrinsically empty pure space of Mind in its Essence.

So in regard to the monkeys and the SLAT you see that the created world's not real because of the original absurdity, triviality, and mere figure of speech which is creation itself and all its so-called Glory and you see no reason to involve your pure realization of your Mind in its Essence and Purity and Primal Nature of Nothingness with any of it.

For by abiding with the unchangeable and Unborn and eternally As-Is, you escape the illusion of great suffering inherent & implicit in changes and the suffering conceptions of existence (birth) and non-existence (death), which is but the life and death, the coming & going, of ideas about form in the Mind, ideas that in Mind Essence are seen as not being real in the least, of course, and are seen as only ideas and conceptions completely empty of self-nature and absolutely ungraspable just like things in dreams.

Why allow your pure and Original essence of Mind, which is in your possession because Mind in its Essence pervades everywhere throughout phenomena in all dimensions and spaces and directions

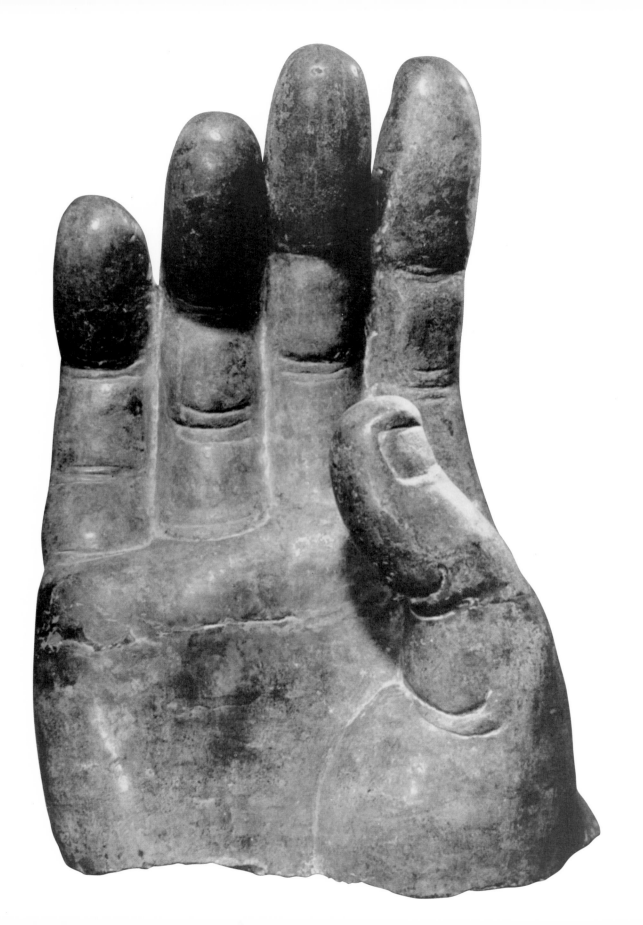

forever without beginning or end, in emptiness, purity, and formless slatless unity, to become defiled by such illusions of thought as "existence" (appearance of a thought) or "non-existence" (disappearance of a thought.)?

It is with your Wisdom Eye you see this, not Beverly's form-eye; and in truth, there's no Wisdom Eye either, it's only a figure of speech. Mind in its Essence is the only Reality because it is what it is.

And supposing the whole universe were suddenly in all Ten Directions inundated and heaped with SLATS, and afterwards completely denuded of SLATS, of forms? What do you think, O ghost of the world?

Instead of thinking about your life, try sometimes gazing at the True Mind that gives rise to your life's dreamlike appearance in the Void, and if only for a moment your "life" will all go up in smoke and vanish, the suffering and the "joy" that is the reverse side of the same sorrowful thing. How can you ever again be deluded as to the existence or non-existence of phenomena such as life, worlds, someone else, people, or personality, or any of these vain notions?

But if this confuses you, it's because this TEACHING is the highest and final TEACHING, and instead of directing you gradually to it through the elementary stages, I use it as your starting point, and apologize for its incompleteness and vestiges of my own very profound ignorance. But your staring point, your starting point, your staring starting stashing point, should be the same as your final point and goal, and there is really no long road ahead, no road, nothing long, nothing at all, and for that matter *no words.*

The final goal is unqualified happiness, the bliss that never dies.

Buddhahood is like a medicine, it will cure you of a hundred ailments all of which you will see

were apparitions in your mind that you clung to because you failed to consider the Essence of it.

Even physical sicknesses can be cured, thanks to the practice of quiet slow breathing during meditation (Dhyana), which loosens the nerves in your stomach and relaxes the whole body and nerve-system like a soothing bath.

But the ailments in your thinking-mind, the general greed, anger and foolishness that overcomes all living beings in their predicament of incessant need, endless wanting, endless not-getting, they too will be cured as you ascend the stages to Holiness in the Contemplation of Essence.

When you will know, remembering as if waking from a dream, the ailments in the thinking-mind (the brain, the thought-maker), they alone were the cause of Suffering, you will know the Knowledge of the Buddhas of Old.

One thing the Lord Buddha preaches: Suffering, and the End of Suffering.

One thing the Lord Buddha gives:- the Path that leads to the end of Suffering.

This path is an ancient path trod by sentient creatures more numerous than the grains of dust in all the universes.

And in Truth, there is no path, no sentient creatures, no universes at all. Isnt this Bright Essential News the greatest thing to Know?

EARNESTNESS

Earnestness is the immortal path,
Carelessness the path of death;
The earnest do not die;
'Tis the careless who are like unto the dead.

Those who know this distinctly,
Pandits in earnestness,
Rejoice in earnestness,
Delighting in the lot of the elect.

These meditative ones, persevering,
Ever strong and valiant,
Being wise, attain Nirvana,
Yoga-calm supreme.

The glory groweth
Of one who is aroused and recollecting,
Clean of deed, considerate in his doing,
Restrained, righteous in life, and earnest.

By rousing himself, by earnestness,
Restraint and temperance,
Let the wise man make himself an island
Which no flood can overwhelm.

EVIL

Let one hasten unto goodness,
And from evil keep his heart:
If one do right perfunctorily,
His mind delights in wrong.

If a man do wrong,
Let him not do it repeatedly;
Let him not take pleasure therein:
Painful is wrong's accumulation.

If a man do right,
Let him do it again and again;
Let him take pleasure therein:
Happiness is an accumulation of right.

Opposite: Buddha statues and tourists. Longmen Caves, Henan, near Luoyang,
China.

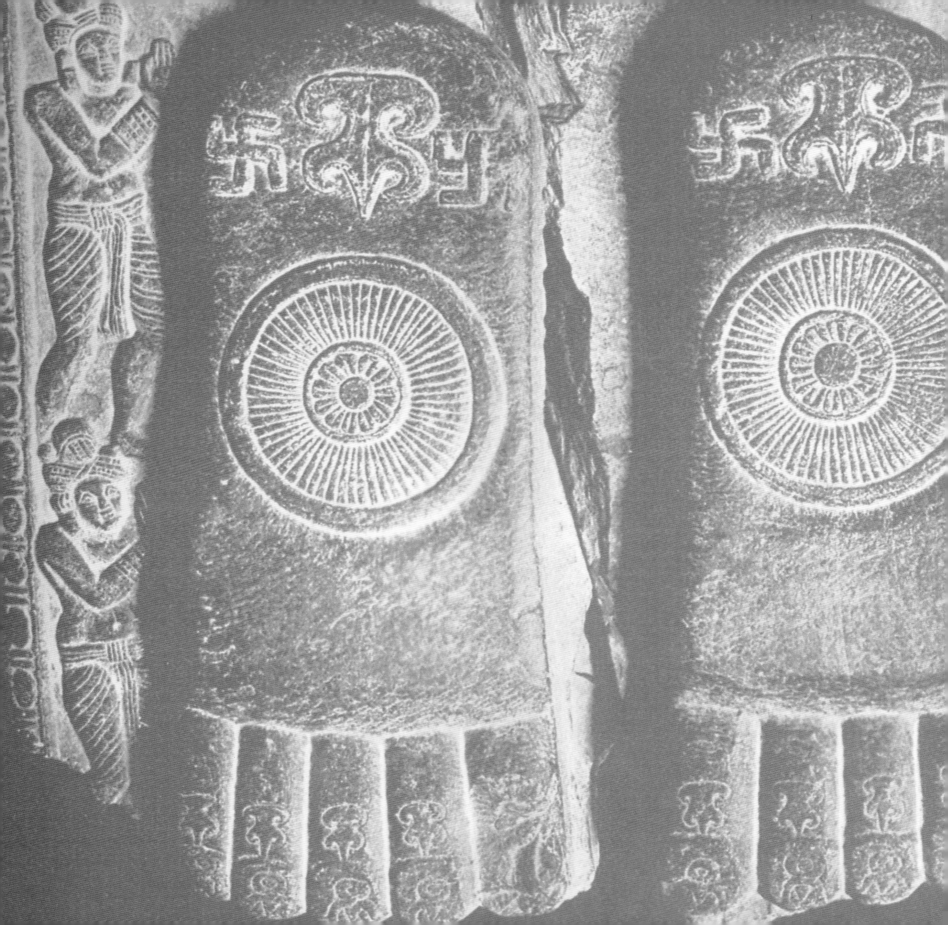

Even an evil man seeth good
So long as evil ripeneth not;
But when ripeneth the evil,
Then seeth he evil things.

Even a good man seeth evil,
So long as goodness ripeneth not;
But when ripeneth the goodness,
Then good things doth he see.

OLD AGE

What laughter now, what joy
In being always on fire?
In darkness wrapped, ye will not seek a light.

Behold [this] variegated figure,
[This] congested body of wounds;
Ailing, with many a resolve,
It hath not firmness or stability.

Wasted this form, a nest of disease, and frail;
Broken the mass of foulness,
For life at the end is death.

What are these things like gourds
In autumn tossed away?
White bones: when seen, what delight?

Of bones is made the citadel,
With mortar of flesh and blood
Wherein are stowed away old age,
Death, pride and hypocrisy!

Opposite: Wooden Buddha. Nara, Japan. Following pages: Reclining Buddha at Wat Pho Temple, Bangkok, Thailand.

THE BUDDHA

One there is whose conquest is reconquered not,
Whose conquest no one in the world can win:
The Buddha, infinite in sphere
And pathless. Him by what path will ye lead?

One there is whom no ensnaring poisonous
desire can lead astray:
The Buddha, infinite in sphere
And pathless. Him by what path will ye lead?

The wise, on trance intent,
Glad with renunciation's calm,
Those real Buddhas, with collected minds,
The very gods do envy.

Hard is the conception of a man,
Hard is the life of mortals,
Hard the hearing of the Gospel,
Hard the arising of the Buddhas.

Ceasing to do all wrong,
Initiation into goodness,
Cleansing the heart:
This is the religion of the Buddhas.

HAPPINESS

Ah! Live we happily in sooth,
Unangered 'mid the angry;
'Mid angry men let us unangered live.

Ah! Live we happily in sooth,
Unailing 'mid the ailing;
'Mid ailing men let us unailing live.

Ah! Live we happily in sooth,
Without greed among the greedy;
'Mid greedy men let us live free from greed.

Ah! Live we happily in sooth,—
We who have nothing:
Feeders on joy shall we be,
Even as the Angels of Splendour.

Victory breedeth anger,
For in pain the vanquished lieth:
Lieth happy the man of peace,
Renouncing victory and defeat.

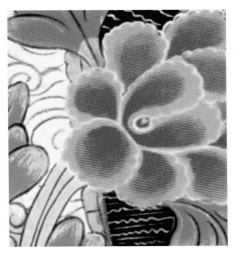

8. The Buddha Enters Nirvana

A. FERDINAND HEROLD

from *The Life of the Buddha*

It was not the season for trees to bloom, yet the two trees that sheltered the Master were covered with blossoms. The flowers fell gently upon his couch, and from the sky, sweet melodies slowly drifted down.

The Master said to pious Ananda:

"See: it is not the season for flowers, yet these trees have bloomed, and the blossoms are raining down upon me. Listen: the air is joyous with the songs that the happy Gods are singing in the sky in honor of the Buddha. But the Buddha is paid a more enduring honor than this. Monks, nuns, believers, all those who see the truth, all those who live within the law, they are the ones that do the Buddha supreme honor. Therefore you must live according to the law, Ananda, and, even in the most trivial matters, you must follow the sacred path of truth."

Ananda was weeping. He walked away, to hide his tears.

He thought, "For many misdeeds I have not yet been forgiven, and I shall be guilty of many more misdeeds. Oh, I am still far from the saintly goal, and he who took pity on me, the Master, is about to enter nirvana."

The Master called him back and said:

Opposite: The dying body of Buddha surrounded by his followers. On the left close to the figure of Buddha stands Indra holding a thunderbolt in his left hand.

Above: Detail of Tibetan thangka painting.

"In what is now known as Bodh Gaya—still a pastoral land of cattle savanna, shimmering water, rice paddies, palms, and red-clay hamlets without paved roads or wires—a Buddhist temple stands beside an ancient pipal, descended from that bodhi tree, or "enlightenment tree," beneath which [Shakyamuni] sat. Here in a warm dawn, ten days ago, with three Tibetan monks in maroon robes, I watched the rising of the morning star and came away no wiser than before. But later I wondered if the Tibetans were aware that the bodhi tree was murmuring with gusts of birds, while another large pipal, so close by that it touched the holy tree with many branches, was without life. I make no claim for this event: I simply declare what I saw there at Bodh Gaya."

— Peter Matthiessen, *The Snow Leopard*

"Do not grieve, Ananda, do not despair. Remember my words: from all that delights us, from all that we love, we must one day be separated. How can that which is born be other than inconstant and perishable? How can that which is born, how can that which is created, endure forever? Long have you honored me, Ananda; you have been a devoted friend. Yours was a happy friendship, and you were faithful to it in thought, in word, and in deed. You have done great good, Ananda; continue in the right path, and you will be forgiven your former misdeeds."

Night came on. The inhabitants of Kusinagara had heard that the Master was reclining under two twin trees, and they came in great crowds to pay him homage. An aged hermit, Subhadra, appeared, and bowing before the Master, professed his belief in the Buddha, in the law, and in the community; and Subhadra was the last of the faithful to have the joy of seeing the Master face to face.

The night was beautiful. Ananda was seated beside the Master. The Master said:

"Perhaps, Ananda, you will think, 'We no longer have a Master.' But you must not think that. The law remains, the law that I taught you; let it be your guide, Ananda, when I shall no longer be with you."

He said again:

"Verily, O monks, all that is created must perish. Never cease to struggle."

He was no longer of this world. His face was of luminous gold. His spirit ascended to the realms of ecstasy. He entered nirvana. The earth shook, and thunder rolled across the sky.

Near the ramparts, at dawn, they of Kusinagara built a great funeral pile, as though for a king of the world, and there they burned the body of the Blessed One.

Opposite: Interior of the Jain Temple at Dila War, showing intricate carving in stone.

9. Boardroom Buddhism

RIGHT LIVELIHOOD: A MODERN FOLD OF THE EIGHTFOLD PATH

ROBERT A. F. THURMAN

After Prince Siddhartha attained enlightenment and became the Buddha, he is said to have given his first teaching to five ascetics. He offered them the famous four noble truths: that the unenlightened life is one of suffering; that suffering originates from misknowledge and misdirected emotions; that freedom from suffering—nirvana—is attainable; and that there is an eightfold path to that freedom.

This teaching became the basis of a peaceful revolution that changed his society, a revolution in which the aims of pleasure, wealth, power, duty, and piety toward the divine were superseded by that of total freedom from suffering—the supreme happiness that every being wants. This revolution brought about not only a change in philosophy, but also a change in ethics and religious institutions.

It is less well known that before the Buddha taught the ascetics, he met two merchants, Trapusha and Bhallika, whose carts had become enmired while they were taking a caravan of luxury goods to market. While waiting for their servants to dig them out, they followed a light coming from deeper in the woods and met with the newly enlightened Buddha, who was glowing with the supreme bliss of perfect understanding. They sent back to their caravan for a delicious repast of rice and ghee and honey to give to the sage as an offering, and they received his blessing. He told them that their affairs would prosper mightily if they continued the practice of supporting seekers of enlightenment. He

Opposite: The Great Buddha at Kamakura, Japan, dates from 1252. Height 49 feet and 7 in. Weight 93 tons. Bronze.
Above: King Ajatasattu visits Buddha. From the Stupa of Bharhut, Madhya Pradesh, India. Second century B.C.E. Three stages of the visit of the king to Buddha are shown, as described in the Samannaphala-sutta.

> "The Buddha's new teaching rejected the belief that birth conferred status automatically, saying that education, ethical excellence, spiritual development, and intellectual understanding are what make a person noble and holy—and that the lack of those qualities makes a person less than a human should be."

gave them some magical spells to recite to avoid getting stuck in the mud in the future, and sent them happily on their way. Of the four noble truths, he did not breathe a word.

The Buddha was originally from the warrior class and the five ascetics were from the priest class; these were the dominant classes in that day. The merchant class was up-and-coming, but the caste societal structure dictated by the Hindu tradition placed them in the lowest rank of the twice-born (though they were far higher than the only once-born laboring class).

The Buddha's new teaching rejected the belief that birth conferred status automatically, saying that education, ethical excellence, spiritual development, and intellectual understanding are what make a person noble and holy—and that the lack of those qualities makes a person less than a human should be. In the Buddha's eightfold path to freedom, which began from "realistic understanding" and ended with "realistic meditative realization," he included "realistic livelihood" and "realistic enterprise." These were defined as the modes of livelihood that minimized violence and maximized benefit, and the modes of creative activity that led to positive physical, moral, mental, and spiritual evolution.

The merchants, who already knew that enterprise, not class, was the key to rising in the world, found this teaching to their liking. They enthusiastically took to their role as patrons of the Buddhist social revolution: The first Buddhist monastery was donated by a fabulously wealthy merchant, Anathapindada, who bought a twenty-acre pleasure garden from Prince Jeta of Rajagrha, covered all but ten square meters with gold coins, built residence halls to protect the monks from the monsoon rains, and presented the Jeta Garden Abode to the monastic community.

Buddhism has since spread all over Asia—and, lately, all over the world—without any crusades. A large part of the quiet success of this continuing peaceful revolution must be attributed to Buddhism's popularity with the merchant classes, and its continuing compatibility with today's business-dominated culture.

Opposite above: Head of the Buddha. Stone. Twelfth century C.E. Khmer, Cambodia. Opposite below: Detail of Buddha head. Forty-eight inches high, bronze. Bar Harbor, Maine, U.S.

121

At birth, Prince Siddhartha was prophesied to become either a world-conqueror or a Buddha, and his father made every effort to see to it that the former destiny would come to pass. He was raised to be a warrior and a leader of warriors—a king. In renouncing his throne and setting forth to attain enlightenment, he betrayed his class and created a new, classless profession—that of the monastic philosopher sage, neither priest nor warrior, a man or woman truly without rank.

The businessmen of his time, the merchant classes, felt a natural affinity with this new order of individualists. They fully appreciated that education makes the man, that enterprise creates a life of value, and that there are no limits on what humans can achieve when free of the artificial constraints imposed by political or religious authorities and the traditions that support them.

When Buddha "awoke," he realized that perfecting the human understanding of reality is the only way to achieve happiness. Merely maintaining one's faith and following dogmatic rules will not do the job. Therefore, he saw his task as founding an educational movement to develop reason and insight, rather than a religious movement that would be reliant on faith and obedience. Buddha rejected indoctrination of any kind and urged people to think for themselves—encouraging them to rely on their own enterprise and intelligence to achieve their own liberation and fulfillment.

Religious scholar B. Alan Wallace, in his writings on the Tibetan education system, has linked this driving force of the Buddha's teachings to the Tibetan curriculum. Students are trained very early on in dialectical thinking through rigorous, judged debate so that their minds become agile, flexible, and capable of profound insight; only after honing the ability to think critically are they immersed in Buddhist teachings.

Opposite: Row of outdoor Buddhas at Boddhi-Tataung near Monywa, Myanmar (Burma).

This educational philosophy appealed mightily to the merchant classes of Asia, with their pragmatic bent and their belief that people can make of themselves whatever they have the courage, persistence, and cleverness to achieve.

This movement of the Buddha, which I have called his "inner revolution," transmitted its influence and resonated with powerful movements all around Eurasia. His near-contemporaries from the East to the West were the luminaries of the "Axial Age" (as historian Arnold J. Toynbee and others called it) of the middle of the first millennium B.C.E.: Socrates, Plato, Deutero-Isaiah, Zoroaster, many other Indian sages, and, further east, Lao-tzu and Confucius. Socrates was poisoned by the Athenians for "corrupting youth"—that is, educating young warriors and encouraging them to think about something more than fighting. Plato's Academy was repeatedly banned by various tyrants. Supported by the Achaemenid imperial state, Isaiah became a high priest, as did Zoroaster; hence both were forced to legitimize warrior culture. Lao-tzu was a librarian who retired from service to his country, the highly militarized Chou dynasty in its warring states period, after he reluctantly gave his profound teachings in The Way and Its Power. Confucius, the father of the mandarinate (the bureaucratized intelligentsia of the Chinese state), was never secure as a mandarin himself; he never held a steady job for any government, and taught his few disciples in his kitchen. Centuries later, Jesus Christ was killed by priests and kings for his teaching that the kingdom of God lies within each individual. The priestly and warrior classes have always been afraid of transcendentalistic individualism.

Only the Buddha survived the intrigues and attacks of his enemy (in his case, his jealous half-brother, Devadatta), and he spent forty-six years giving his teachings to priests, kings, merchants, and even women and the laboring classes. He founded an educational institution that flourished in the sixteen nations of north India during his lifetime and spread so rapidly after his passing that within a few centuries the Mauryan emperor Ashoka proclaimed Buddhism as the national religion of India. Arnold Toynbee, in

his voluminous *A Study of History,* singled out the Buddha as the most successful of the great ethical and intellectual teachers of this pivotal age. Toynbee further observed that it was the comparatively greater wealth of India, created especially by its merchant classes, that made such success possible.

The Buddhist revolution, then, marked the beginning of a global process that has lasted for thousands of years: the shift of power and status from the warrior to the merchant class. It was clear to the Buddha that trade and exchange was preferable to war and pillage as a method of creating wealth; with the latter, one violently takes things and territory from others, or destroys them, whereas with the former, one negotiates with the other and exchanges one's things of value for other things of value, continuing that process in unlimited expansion, leaving the other alive and even enriched to trade with again another day.

This process is not yet complete, however. The modern phrase "military-industrial complex" tends to confuse the global trend involved, by implying that industrialism and militarism are indistinguishable. Granted, the sometimes militaristic, often sports-inspired ethos of today's megacorporations has been encouraged by our century's addiction to warfare, leading to the focus on a very short-term bottom line. But the shortest-term bottom line approach—conquering the consumer and taking everything he has—leads to destruction of your customers. Sooner or later, that puts you out of business.

After the United States helped Japan and Germany get back on their feet after the last world war, both countries pulled ahead of the war's victors by putting their creativity into consumer industries instead of military ones. Today, America is thriving in large part because it has shifted its technological development from arms proliferation into biotechnology and information-processing industries. When the Internet becomes better understood, it might indeed change American attitudes about the connections between peacetime and prosperity.

Our current fascination with Buddhism goes beyond fad and fashion. We maybe gradually recognizing the downside of our violence-prone lifestyle, which not only drains our national budget but infects our households, schools, neighborhoods, theaters, diets, hospitals, and television sets.

At the same time, we seem to be learning to enjoy the upside of our creative business culture, which brings greater pleasure, comfort, health, and knowledge within our reach. Buddhists consider true happiness to be a realistically attainable goal of human life and applaud the creation of wealth as the foundation that makes possible the institutional and individual efforts to attain that goal. The dawn of the twenty-first century may, in fact, be the ideal moment for business to recognize the long history, and long-term market potential, of awakening.

127

10. Awaiting Execution, and Finding Buddha

KEVIN SACK
from *The New York Times*

TUCKER, Ark., May 27—William Frank Parker, a double murderer with a nasty habit of slugging corrections officers, was doing time in solitary confinement one day when he asked a prison guard, somewhat impolitely, for a Bible to read.

The guard, his sense of humor stimulated by Mr. Parker's insolence, opened the cell door, tossed in a copy of a Buddhist tract known as the Dhammapada, and slammed the door shut. Mr. Parker, with little else to do, began to read.

Seven years later, Mr. Parker is the only practicing Buddhist in the Arkansas prison system. And as his appointment with a lethal injection approaches, he has become a cause celebre among Buddhists worldwide. Earlier this month, the Dalai Lama himself joined the hundreds of clemency-seeking correspondents who have written Gov. Jim Guy Tucker on Mr. Parker's behalf.

Death row conversions are common, but Mr. Parker's seems to be different. His Buddhism, he says, concerns neither salvation nor repentance. It is less a religion than "a transformational psychology" that guides practitioners toward inner peace, a rather scarce commodity on death row.

"The Buddha said the greatest of all footprints is that of the elephant, and the greatest meditation is that on death," Mr. Parker said in an interview at the Maximum Security Unit here, the site of Arkansas's

Opposite: **Buddha.** Above: **Buddha in the gesture of the meditation. About 16.4 feet high. Stone.**

death row. "I needed to come to grips with death. I was having trouble with it. Buddhism teaches that it's the big lie, the big delusion.

"Now I know," he said, pointing to his chest, "that this vehicle will die. But what's in it moves on."

Indeed, the forty-one-year-old Mr. Parker has forbidden his lawyer, Jeffrey M. Rosenzweig of Little Rock, to file additional appeals of his convictions for killing his former wife's parents and wounding his former wife and a police officer in 1984. While he would not object to a commutation of his sentence to life without parole, he says he has no interest in delays of an inevitable execution.

"He has psychologically steeled himself to be executed and has reached a peace of some sort about it and is not sure he wants to disturb that," Mr. Rosenzweig said.

Until a last-minute unrequested reprieve bought him some time, Mr. Parker's execution had been scheduled for Wednesday. On Friday, Governor Tucker delayed the execution until July 11 so the United States Supreme Court would have time to judge the constitutionality of a new Federal law that limits appeals by condemned prisoners.

Many of the clemency pleas written to Mr. Tucker, whether from Buddhist priests in Sri Lanka or Zen masters in Honolulu, cite Mr. Parker's rededication of his life to Buddhism. His conversion has been so convincing that many inmates and guards call him by the Buddhist name he assumed several years ago, Si-Fu, which means "master" or "teacher." When he approaches, some bow, their hands clasped in front of their faces.

Each night, he waits for the rantings of the condemned to fade and then rises at three A.M. to meditate in silence for forty minutes. His cell has become a temple, complete with a brass statuette of the Buddha and, when the warden allows, burning candles and incense. During crackdowns on such possessions, he makes do. "I can make candles," Mr. Parker said. "I can make incense."

He has read dozens of books on Buddhist wisdom and laces his conversations with references to Zen masters, the Bible, and Carl Jung. He has learned to fashion intricate origami flowers and birdcages from paper supplied by his mother. He has shaved his head in devotion and wears a ritualistic black apron over his prison whites. During a recent interview, he wrapped brown prayer beads around his hands while silver cuffs shackled his ankles.

"He has the most impressive understanding of Buddhism of any inmate I've ever met," said Kobutsu Shindo (also known as Kevin C. Malone), a Buddhist priest who ministers to inmates at the Sing Sing Correctional Facility in New York and the leader of the campaign to spare Mr. Parker. "And he has as deep an understanding as many Western Buddhist teachers. The man belongs in a monastery, not on death row."

Even Mr. Parker's mother, Janie N. Parker of Bastrop, Tex., who has had reasons for skepticism about her son over the years, said she was convinced of the depth of his conversion. "I thought it might be a fake at first because so many of them get jailhouse religion," Mrs. Parker said. "But the longer I talked to him, the more I realized he was into it."

Mr. Parker said the religion seized him when he read Buddha's teachings that impure thoughts led to trouble. "I said, This is me here," he recalled. "I knew that my own crimes, my own history, I had acted with an impure heart."

His education has not always been easy. When a prison chaplain refused his orders of Buddhist books, Mr. Parker threatened to throw him over a second-floor railing. "I know it was anti-Buddhist to say that," Mr. Parker said, adding, "Now I don't have any problems."

On Nov. 5, 1984, Mr. Parker, high on liquor and cocaine, and desperately unhappy about his recent divorce, killed his former in-laws at their house in Rogers, Ark., and later abducted his former wife. For reasons he says he cannot now fathom, he took her to a police station where he shot her and wounded

"Kobutsu Shindo visited Mr. Parker and performed a jukai ceremony, a high-level initiation into Buddhism during which Mr. Parker received a new name, Ju San, or 'mountain of everlasting life.' An abbot's inscription on a certificate encouraged him to 'depart with dignity like a mountain, trusting that his life is everlasting.'"

a policeman three times before being disarmed. His lawyer's efforts to appeal the convictions, mostly on the ground of double jeopardy, have been unsuccessful.

At a state clemency board hearing earlier this month, a prosecutor said that Mr. Parker once joked that he had turned the Warrens into "worm food." His former wife, Pamela Warren Bratcher, told board members, "Frankie Parker has been given eleven and a half more years than he gave my parents." The board voted five to zero to advise the Governor not to commute Mr. Parker's sentence.

Mr. Parker said that he was remorseful, but that he had not written Ms. Bratcher because any apology would be inadequate. "What are you going to do?" he asked. "Say, 'Sorry I killed your Mom and Dad?'"

But he also mocks Ms. Bratcher's devotion to his demise. "My death is her life," he said, "and when I die, she's going to be lost."

On Saturday, Kobutsu Shindo visited Mr. Parker and performed a jukai ceremony, a high-level initiation into Buddhism during which Mr. Parker received a new name, Ju San, or "mountain of everlasting life." An abbot's inscription on a certificate encouraged him to "depart with dignity like a mountain, trusting that his life is everlasting."

Mr. Parker said he would do so.

"My friends on death row used to say, 'If you think those Buddhists are going to get you off death row, forget it. Those Buddhists love death,'" he said. "I don't want to die. But I'm ready. In fact, I'm sort of looking forward to the journey. I've studied it for so long."

Seated Buddha. Sandstone.
Fifth century C.E. Sarnath,
India. National Museum,
New Delhi.

135

A Buddhist Timeline

• 560 to 480 BCE
Life of Siddhartha Gautama

• 479 CE
First Council results in four
factions one year after
Buddha's death.

• 469 CE
Approximately sixteen factions
ten years after Buddha's
death

• 390 BCE
Second Council declares a
minority orthodox
(Hinayana) and the
majority heretic
(Mahayana).

• 297 BCE
King Asoka of India converts
to Buddhism. It grows
from small group to state
religion and local religion
to world religion as Asoka
sends out Buddhist
missionaries.

• 247 BCE
Asoka calls Third Council to
agree on authentic
Buddhist scriptures.

• First century BCE
Construction of the great
Stupa at Sanchi

• First century CE
Buddhism splinters into
perhaps as many as 500
sects.

• 200 BCE to 200 CE
Development of Hinayana
Buddhism

• Second century CE
Development of Mahayana
Buddhism

• Third century CE
Expansion of Buddhism to
Burma, Cambodia, Laos,
Vietnam, and Indonesia

Previous pages: Center detail of Tibetan wall hanging.

Opposite: Dafu (Grand Buddha) statue, largest in world, Leshan, Sichuan, China.

- Fourth century CE

Development of Vajrayana
    Buddhism in India
Buddhism enters Korea.
Buddhism and Hinduism
    coexist as one tradition in
    Nepal.

- 480 CE

Bodhidharma travels as a
    Buddhist missionary to
    China.

- Sixth century CE

Buddhism enters Japan.

- Fifth to seventh century CE

Pure Land sects develop in
    China.

- Seventh to ninth century CE

Buddhism moves into Tibet,
    where it struggles with the
    local nature religion,
    Bonism, which claims the
    gods are angry with
    Tibetans for accepting this
    new religion.

- Tenth to fourteenth centuries CE

Buddhism's second revival in
    Tibet; lamaism goes to the
    Mongol court in northern
    China; eleventh century:
    reform of sexual tantric
    tradition.

- Eleventh to thirteenth
    centuries CE

India encounters Islam,
    iconoclasm.

- Twelfth century CE

Moslems attack and conquer
    Magadha, India, in 1193
    destroying the Buddhist
    monasteries and wiping
    out Buddhism in that area.

- Thirteenth century CE

Founding of Pure Land,
    Nichiren, and Zen sects in
    Japan

- 13th century CE

Decline of Buddhism in
    northern India

- 15th century CE

Decline of Buddhism in
    southern India

- Fifteenth century CE

Dalai Lama lineage begins in
    Tibetan Buddhism.

- Sixteenth century CE

Master Ingen (1592–1673)
    founds the Obaku-shu Zen
    school in Japan.

- Seventeenth century CE

(Sri Lanka) Reintroduction of
    Dharma twice from Burma

- 1868–1871 CE

The text of the Pali Canon is
    revised and inscribed on
    729 marble slabs.

- 1905 CE

Zen teachers arrive in North
    America.

- 1920s CE

Soviet Communist attack on
    Buddhism in Mongolia

- 1950 CE

Beginning of Chinese
    Communist attack on
    Buddhism in Tibet.

- 1952 CE

Formation of World
    Fellowship of Buddhists
    Mahayana Sects
    Pure Land

- 1956 CE

Buddha Jayanti celebrations in
    Asia

- 1959 CE

Exodus of Tibetans, including
    His Holiness the Dalai
    Lama, from Tibet.

- 1989 CE

Dalai Lama receives Nobel
    Peace Prize.

The life of Buddha depicted in stone, from the great stupa of Borobudur in Java.

Acknowledgments

This book would not have been possible without the help of the following:
Genevieve Morgan, Jason Gardner, Lelah Cole, Anna Gilbert, Amy Rennert, James A. Morgan, Lama Surya Das, Robert A. F. Thurman, and Glen Allison.

Permissions

Grateful acknowledgment is made for permission to reprint the following:

Principal color photography copyright © 2002 by Glen Allison.

"Enlightenment" is from *Buddha* by Karen Armstrong, copyright © 2001 by Karen Armstrong. Used by permission of Viking Penguin, a division of Penguin Putnam, Inc.

"Sangye Menla," Medicine Buddha of Healing (Stained Glass Thangka), copyright © 2002 by Ani Thubten Jamyang Donma (aka Catherine A. Brock), Yulokod Studios, Toronto, Ontario, Canada, M4W 1W8.

"The Brahmin's Son" is from *Siddhartha* by Hermann Hesse, copyright © 1951 by New Directions Publishing Corp. Reprinted by permission of New Directions Publishing Corp.

"Awaiting Execution, and Finding Buddha" by Kevin Sack, copyright © 1996 by The New York Times Co. Reprinted by permission.

"Boardroom Buddhism" is reprinted by permission of Robert Thurman, copyright © 1999 by Robert Thurman.

Opposite: The Great Phandawgyer Buddha. Stone bricks. Eleventh century C.E. Pagan, Myanmar (Burma). Following page: Buddha under Naga. Stone. From Prachinburi.